The Developing Artist
Artist
Piano Sonatinas

Book Four   Early Advanced

A Comprehensive,
Well-Graded Series
of Authentic
Keyboard Sonatinas.

Compiled and edited by
Nancy and Randall Faber

T0057145

Production: Frank & Gail Hackinson
Production Coordinator: Marilyn Cole
Cover & Illustrations: Terpstra Design, San Francisco
Engraving: GrayBear Music Company, Hollywood, Florida

FABER
PIANO ADVENTURES®

ISBN 978-1-61677-113-3

TABLE OF CONTENTS

SONATINAS

Clementi, Muzio (Op. 36, No. 4) 20

Clementi, Muzio (Op. 36, No. 6) 30

Gurlitt, Cornelius (Op. 54, No. 1) 46

Keller, Oswin 16

Kuhlau, Friedrich (Op. 88, No. 1) 6

Kuhlau, Friedrich (Op. 88, No. 3, 3rd movement) 40

SONATAS

Beethoven, Ludwig van (Op. 49, No. 2) 62

Haydn, Franz Joseph (Hob. XVI/13, 3rd movement) 58

Mozart, Wolfgang Amadeus (K. 545) 73

Mozart, Wolfgang Amadeus (K. 331, 3rd movement: Rondo à la Turk) 86

Understanding Musical Form. 4

About the Composers 96

Dictionary of Musical Terms 92

FF1113

UNDERSTANDING MUSICAL FORM

Musical *form* is a way of organizing or structuring music. The following forms are common in classical sonatinas and sonatas. You and your teacher may wish to refer to this page as you study the pieces in this book.

Binary (2-part) or AB form

The simplest musical form is one section of music followed by another section: **section A** followed by **section B**. Each section usually has a repeat sign. This 2-part (binary) form can be shown like this:

$$\| : \quad A \quad : \| : \quad B \quad : \|$$

Rounded binary form

This is still 2-part form, but with an interesting feature. In rounded binary form, the theme from section **A** returns within the **B** section.

It can be shown like this:

$$\| : \quad A \quad : \| : \quad B \quad (A) \quad : \| \quad \text{(coda optional)}$$

Ternary form (3-part) or ABA form

Ternary means 3-parts: **section A**, **section B**, and the return of **section A**. Ternary form is common in slow, lyric second movements. This 3-part form can be shown like this:

$$A \quad B \quad A \quad \text{(coda optional)}$$

Rondo form

In this form, the **A section** reappears after each new section. Rondo form is common for lively 3rd movements. A typical rondo form looks like this:

$$A \quad B \quad A \quad C \quad A$$

Sonata-allegro form

A more complex form, sonata-allegro form is used for first movements of sonatas and longer sonatinas. Many sonatinas, however, vary from precisely following the form.

In the first section, called the **exposition**, the themes are presented or "exposed."
The 1st theme is usually followed with a more lyrical 2nd theme, usually in the key of the dominant. The exposition may end with a closing theme. The entire exposition is usually repeated.

The middle section is called the **development**. Themes or parts of themes may be presented in new keys or "developed" in imaginative ways. Shorter sonatinas may have only a transitional passage instead of a development section.

The final section is called the **recapitulation**. Here the themes are restated, or "recapped." Both the 1st and 2nd themes appear in the tonic key. Sometimes there are repeat signs at the end of the movement, which go back to the development. These are reminiscent of rounded binary form. It is common performance practice today, however, not to take this repeat.

A *coda* (ending) or *codetta* (short ending) will often end the movement.

Sonata-allegro form can be shown like this:

Exposition
    1st theme (in the tonic)
    2nd theme (in the dominant)
    closing theme (in the dominant)

Development

    Themes are developed. Composers often use the following:
    key changes, frequent accidentals, parts of the theme (motifs),
    repetition, imitation, sequence

Recapitulation
    1st theme (in the tonic)
    2nd theme (in the tonic)
    closing theme (in the tonic)

Coda (optional)

Sonatina
Op. 88, No. 1

Friedrich Kuhlau
(1786-1832)

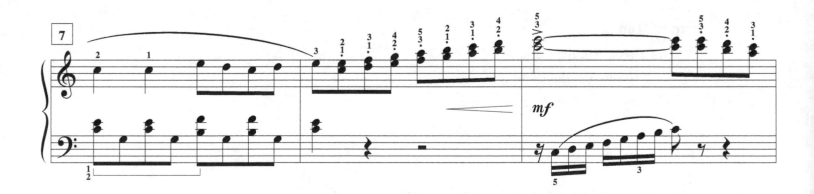

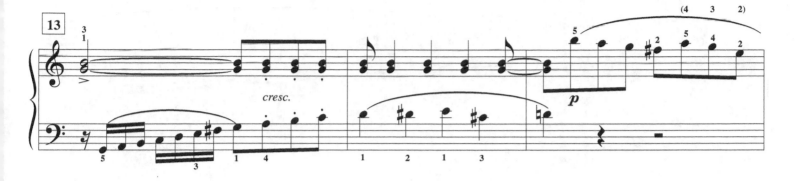

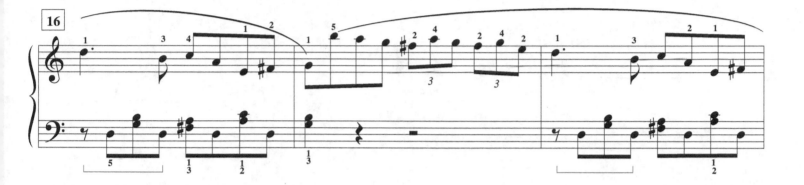

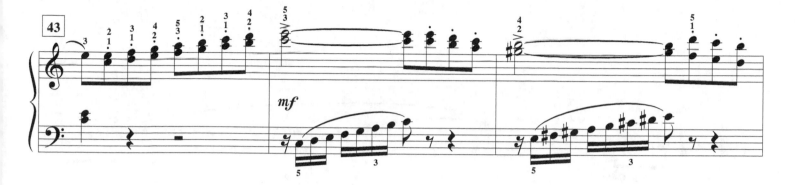

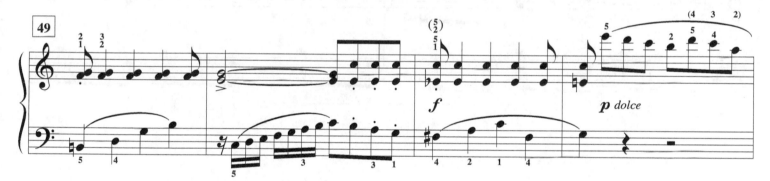

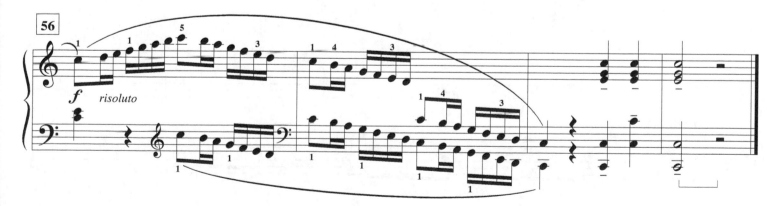

Exploring the Score: Label the **exposition**, **development**, and **recapitulation** in this movement.

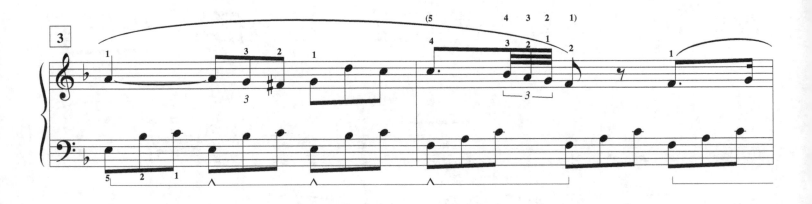

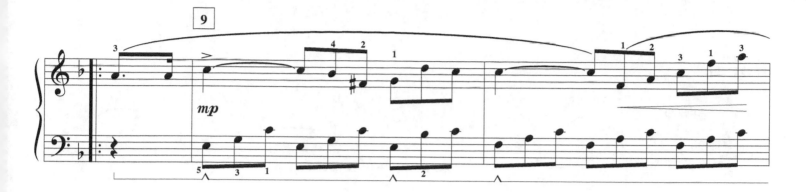

Exploring the Score: Point out the three **cadences** in F major in this slow movement.
Where is the cadence in A minor?

Rondo

14

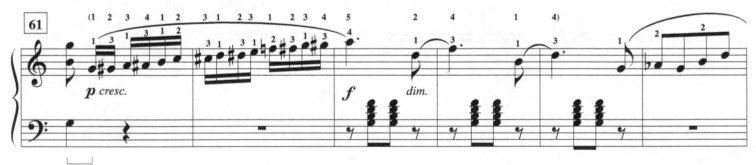

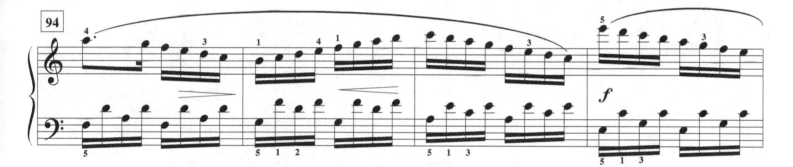

Exploring the Score: Mark the opening **A theme** each time it occurs.

(Hint: It appears five times.)

Sonatina

Oswin Keller
(1885-1928)

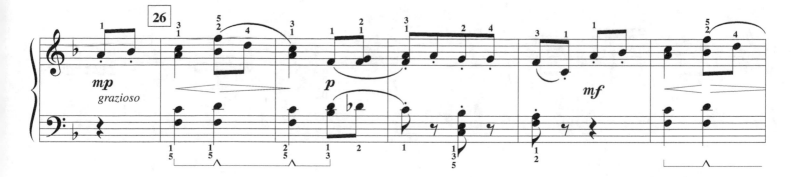

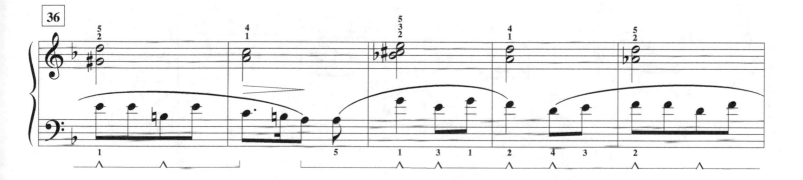

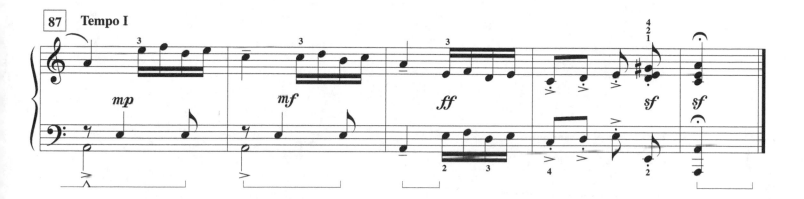

Exploring the Score: Point out 3 cadences on the **V chord** (E major).

Point out at least 4 cadences on the **i chord** in A minor.

Sonatina
Op. 36, No. 4

Muzio Clementi
(1752-1832)

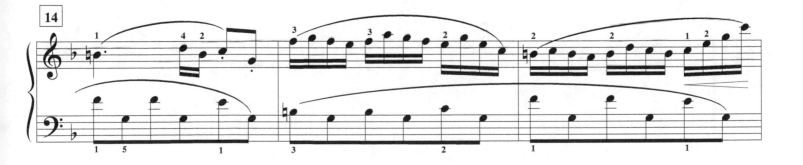

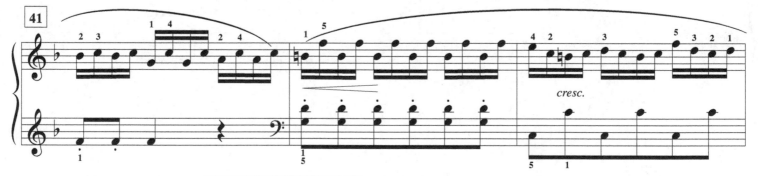

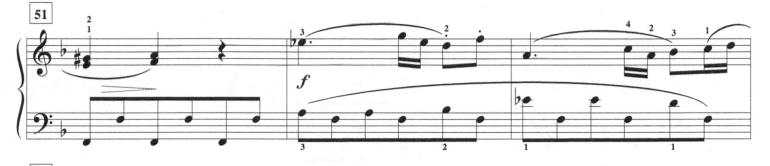

Exploring the Score: Does the development begin in the **tonic** key or **dominant** key? *(circle one)*

Andante con espressione

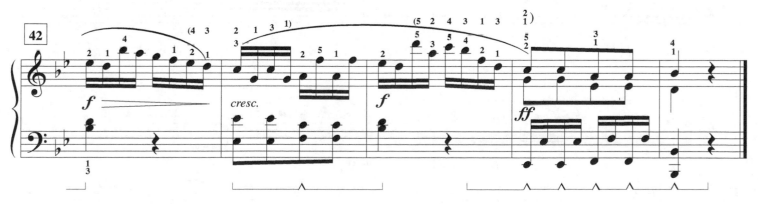

Exploring the Score: Mark each appearance of the opening theme as **A**, **A^1**, **A^2**, or **A^3**.
How is each return of the A section varied?

Allegro vivace

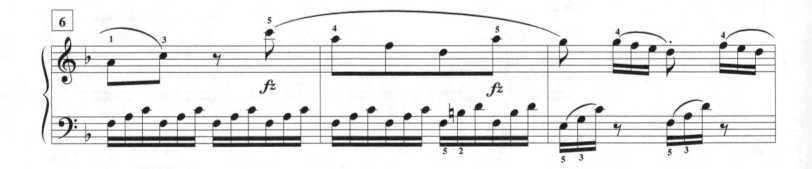

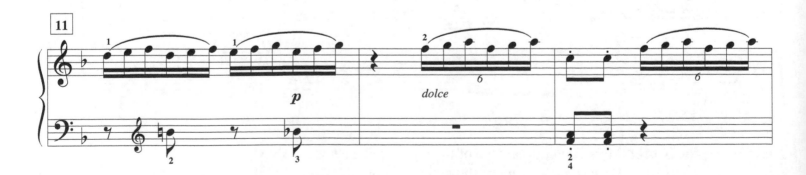

27

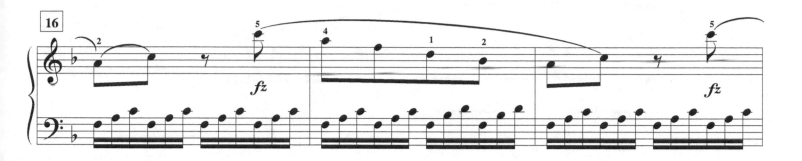

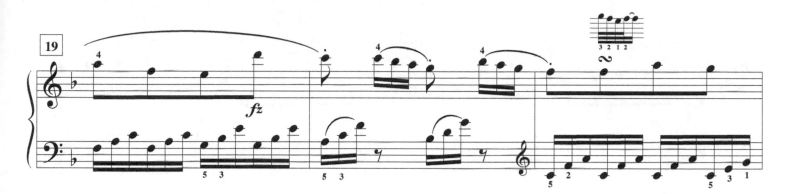

FF1113

28

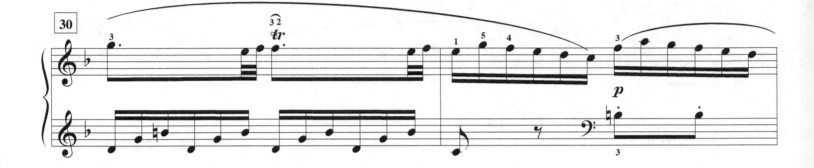

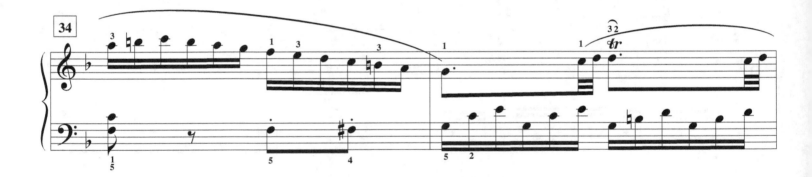

FF1113

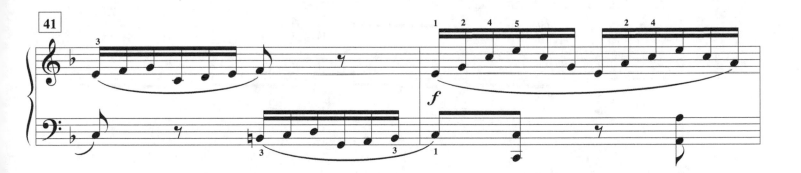

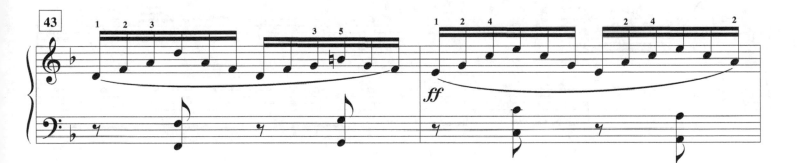

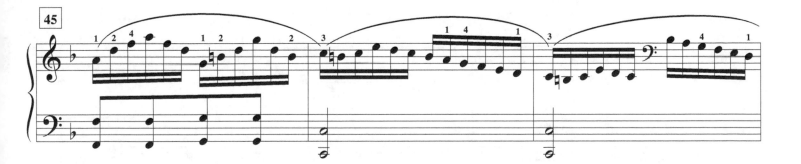

Exploring the Score: How do the pick-up notes into *measure 28* differ from the opening of the movement?

Sonatina
Op. 36, No. 6

Muzio Clementi
(1752-1832)

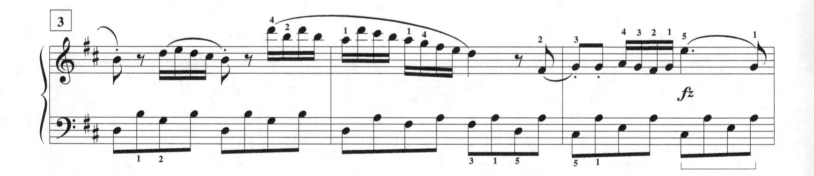

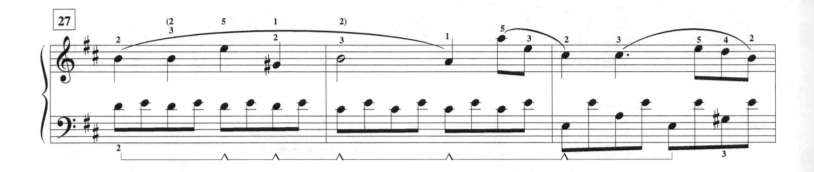

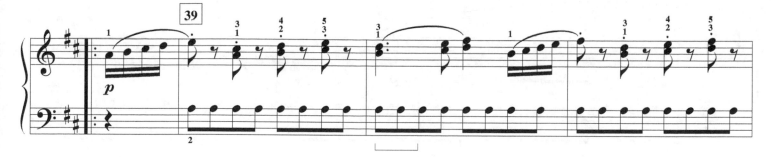

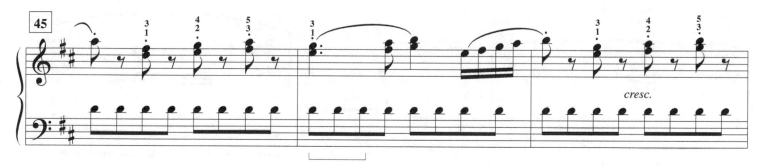

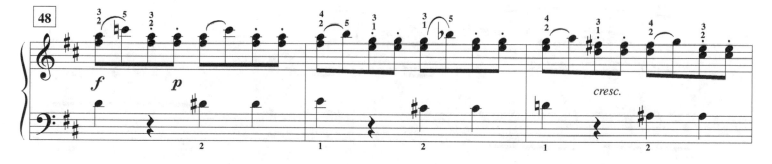

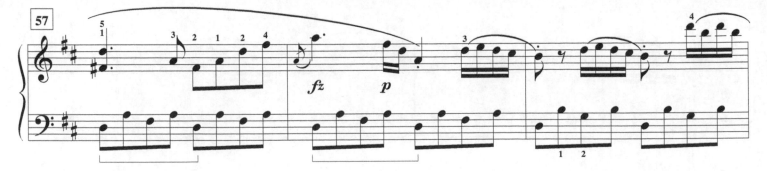

Exploring the Score: Label the **2nd theme** at *measure 23*. Is it in the key of the tonic or dominant?
Find and label the 2nd theme in the recapitulation.
Is it in the key of the tonic or the dominant?

Allegro spiritoso

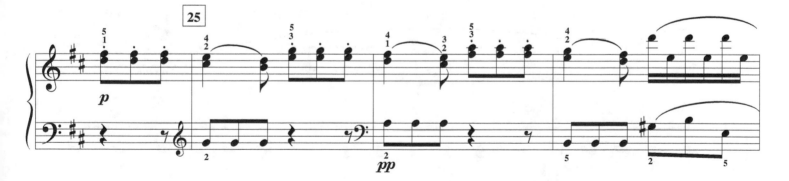

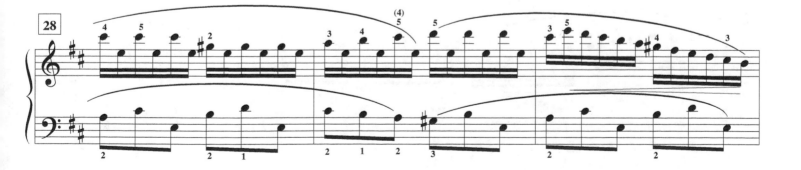

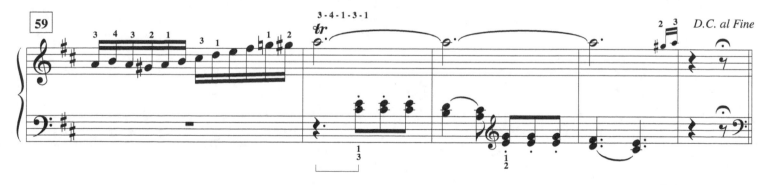

Exploring the Score: Study the **opening theme** from *measure 1-7*.

How does Clementi vary the theme and accompaniment in *measures 8-15?*

Sonatina
Op. 88, No. 3
3rd movement

Friedrich Kuhlau
(1786-1832)

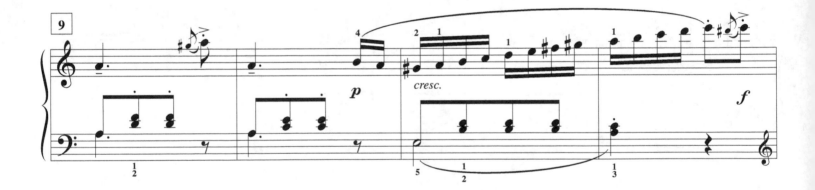

41

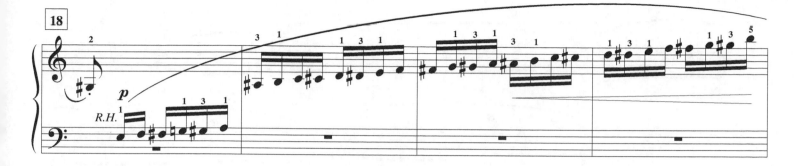

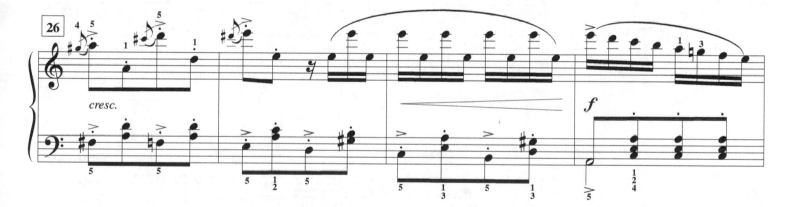

FF1113

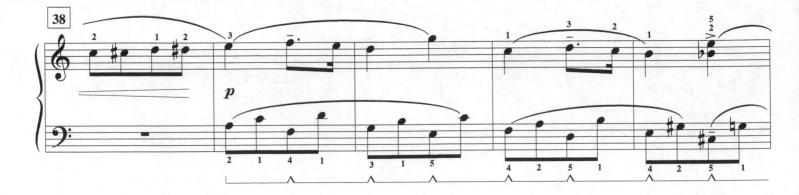

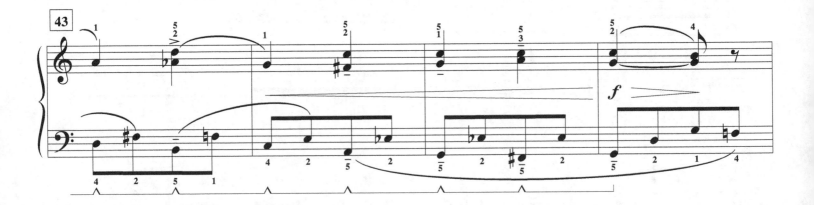

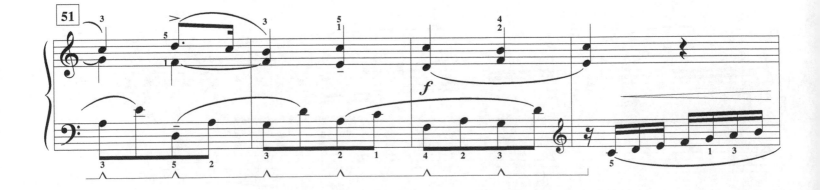

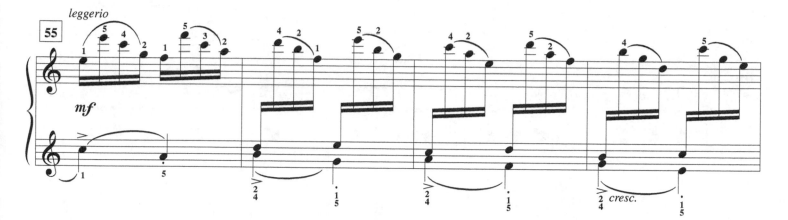

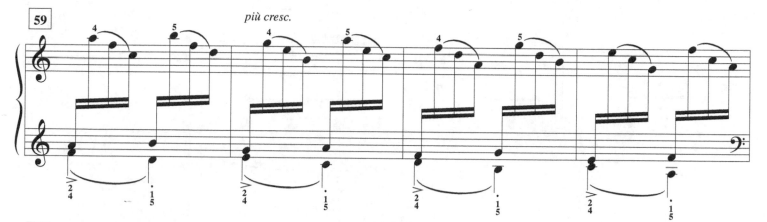

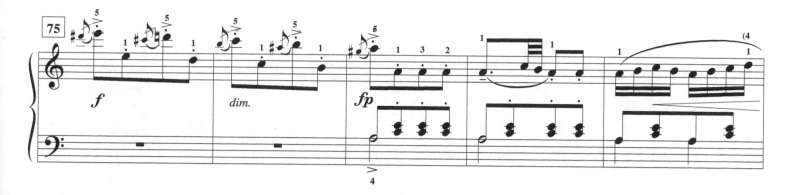

44

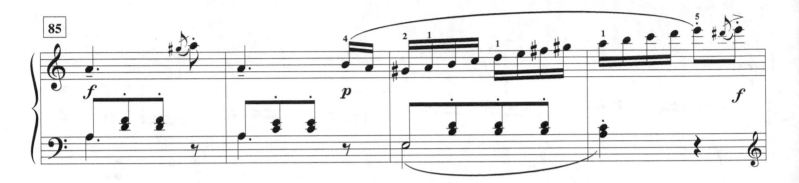

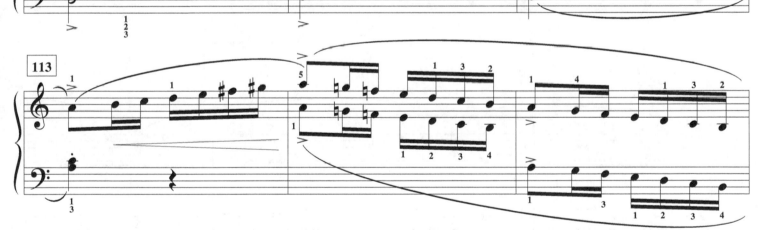

Exploring the Score: The opening 8-measure theme uses only two chords.
Circle the correct answer.

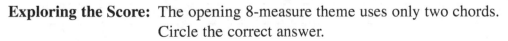

i and **V(7)**   **I** and **V(7)**   **i** and **iv**

Sonatina
Op. 54, No. 1

Cornelius Gurlitt
(1820-1901)

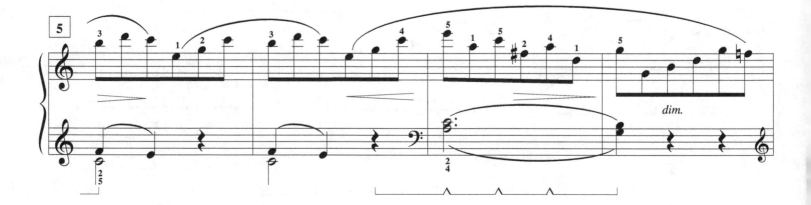

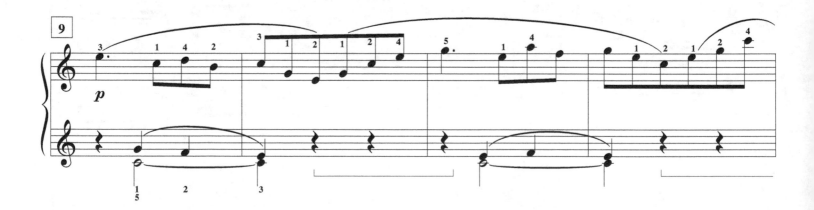

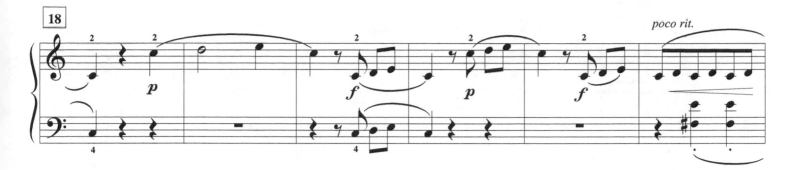

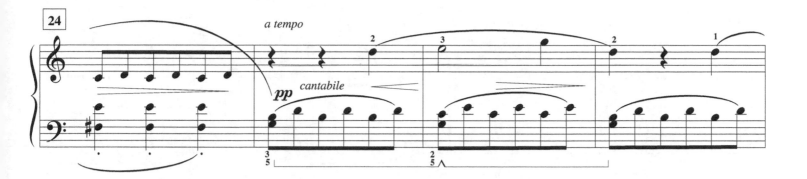

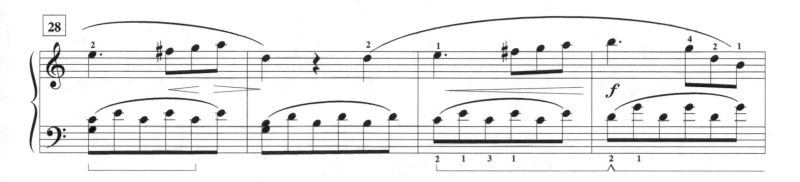

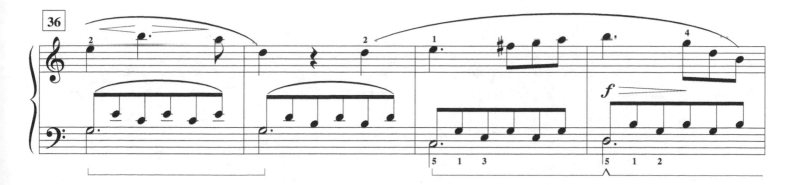

48

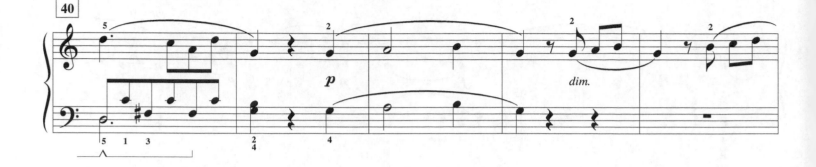

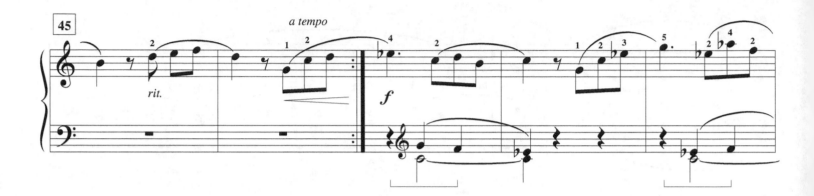

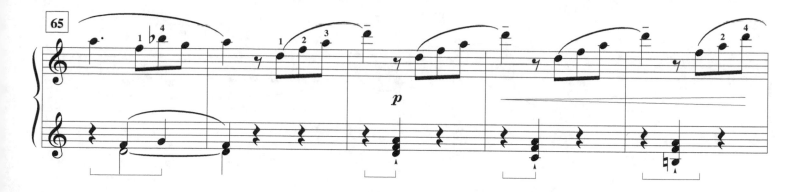

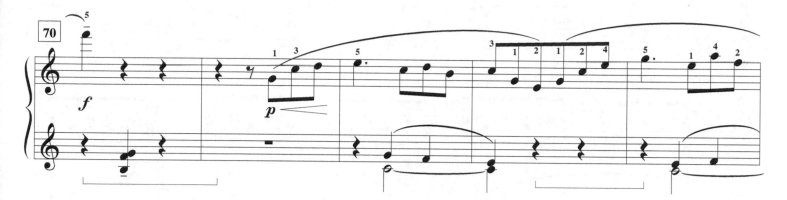

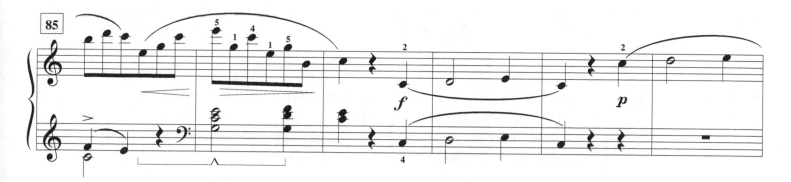

50

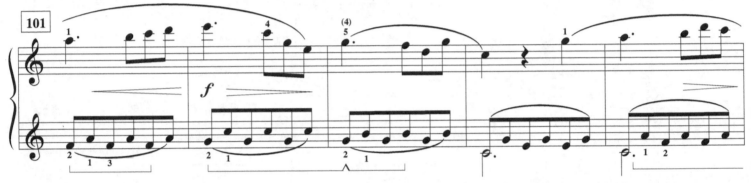

Exploring the Score: The **exposition** consists of a 1st theme, 8-measure transition passage, and 2nd theme. Mark each in your music.

In the **recap**, mark the 1st theme, transition passage, and 2nd theme.

In what key is the 2nd theme?

Adagio non troppo

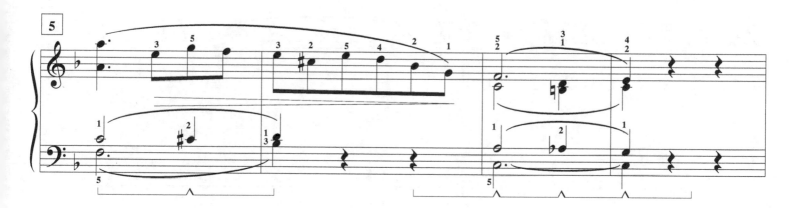

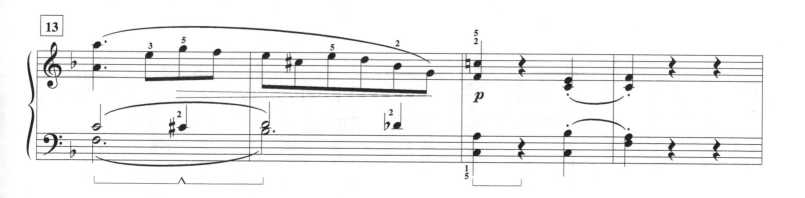

52

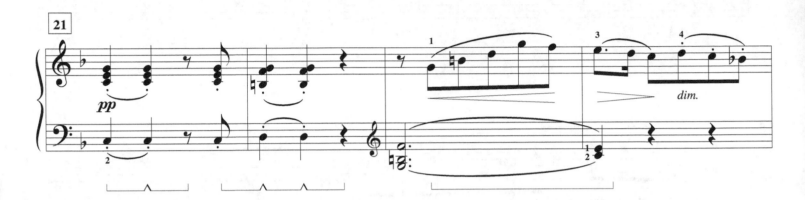

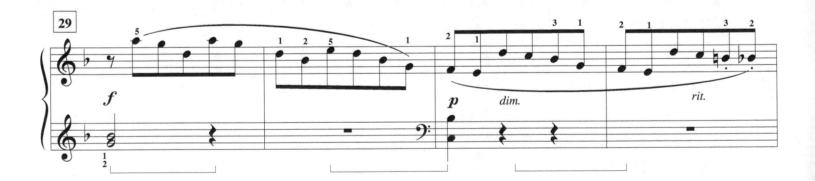

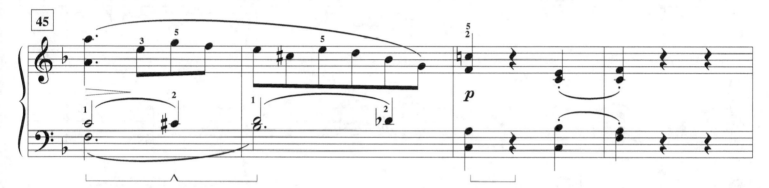

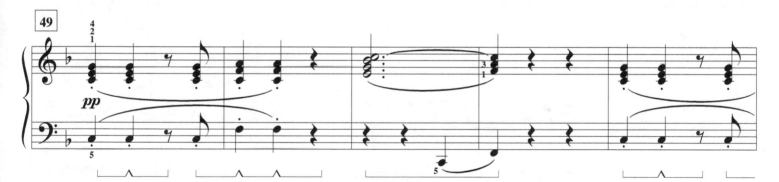

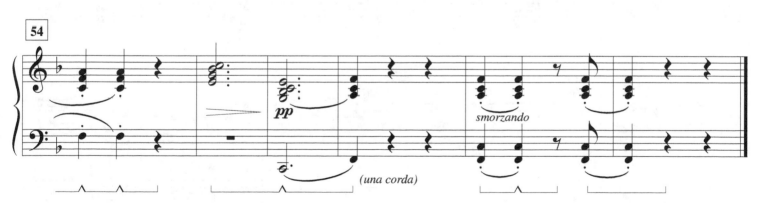

Exploring the Score: This movement uses a repeating one-measure rhythmic *motif* (idea) throughout the piece. Write the rhythm below.

54

Allegretto

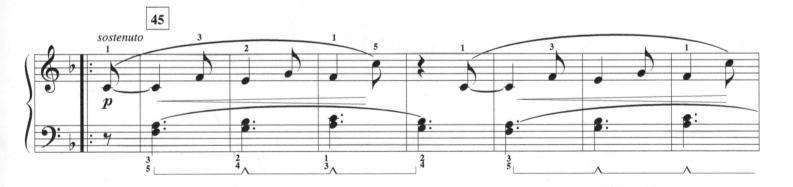

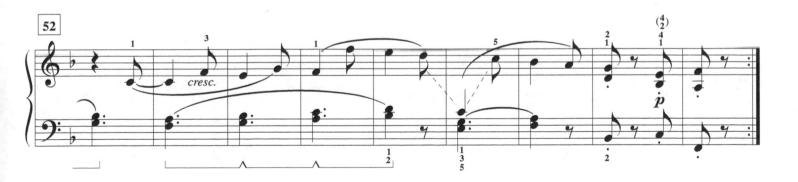

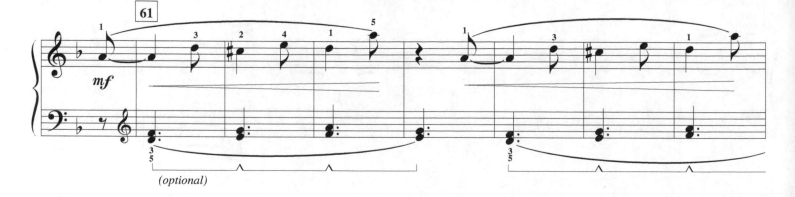

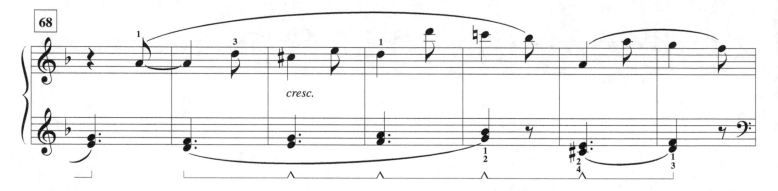

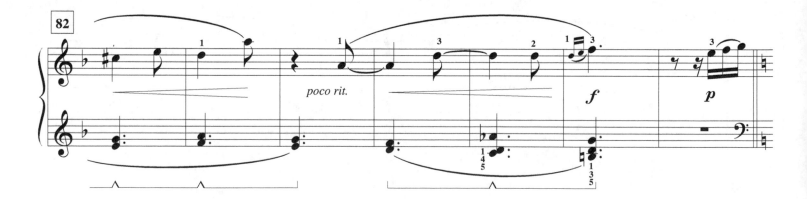

Exploring the Score: The form of the movement is:

        A   **A¹** (slightly different)   **B**   **B¹** (in minor)   **A¹**   **coda**

        Find and label each section in your music.

Sonata
Hob. XVI/13
Third Movement

Franz Joseph Haydn
(1732-1809)

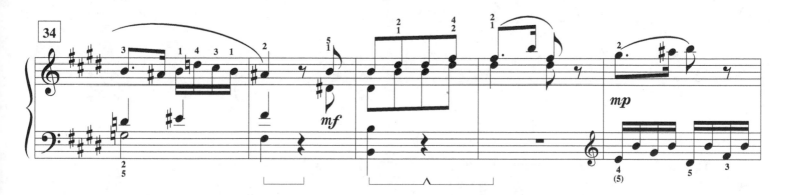

*The appoggiatura *(b)* is played on the beat as a sixteenth note, followed by a *c#-d#* trill.
 The terminating notes are recommended by the editors.

Exploring the Score: In which two ways does *measure 9* give contrast to the opening theme?

1. change in accompaniment   2. change to minor   3. octave change   4. dynamic change

Sonata
Op. 49, No. 2

Ludwig van Beethoven
(1770-1827)

Allegro, ma non troppo

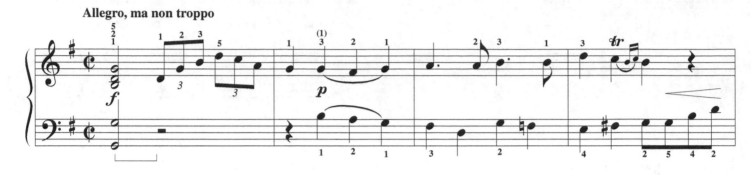

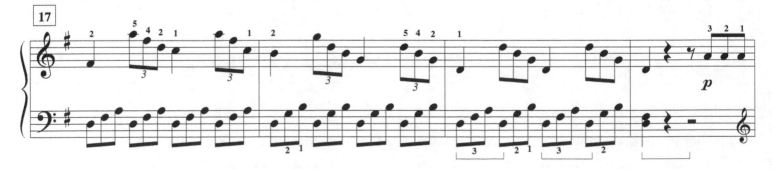

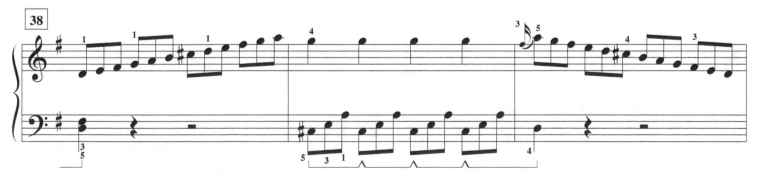

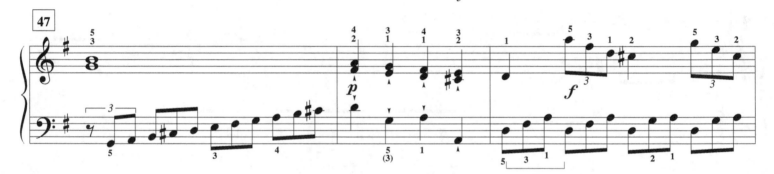

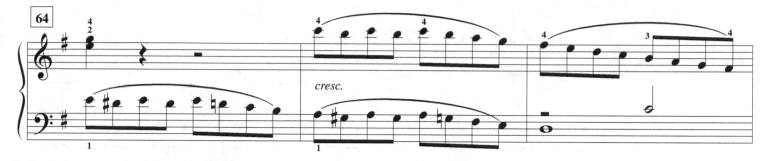

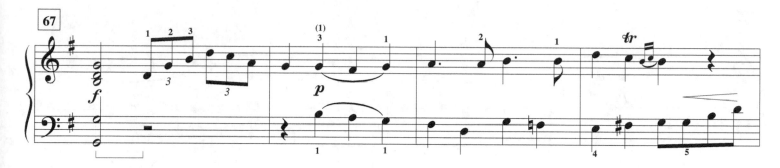

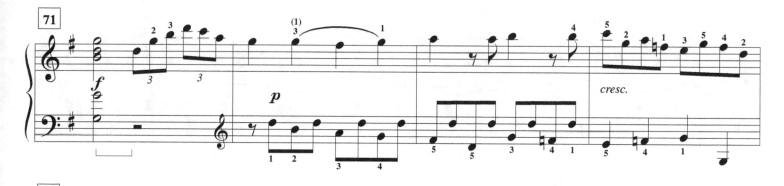

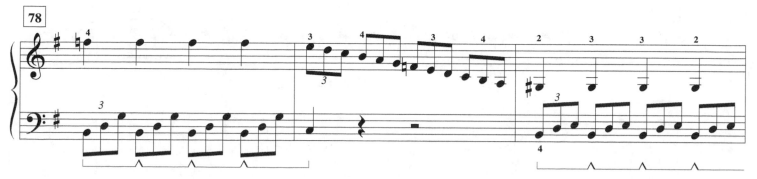

Exploring the Score: Mark the following in your music:

Exposition (1st theme and 2nd theme), Development, Recapitulation (1st theme and 2nd theme)

68

Tempo di Menuetto

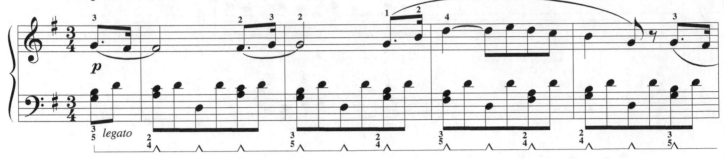

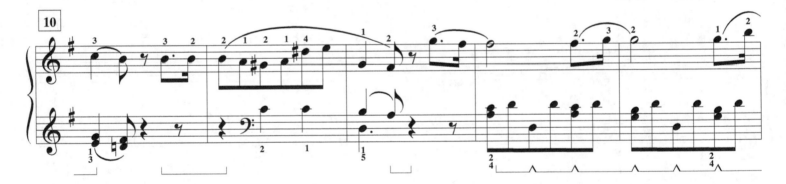

FF1113

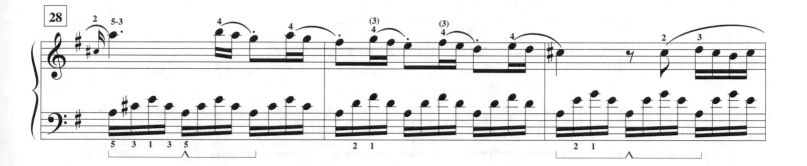

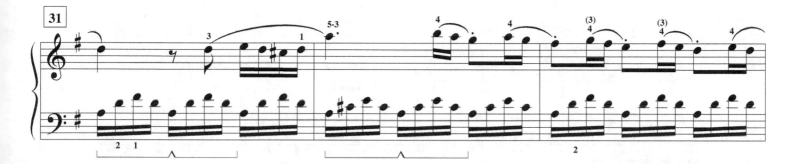

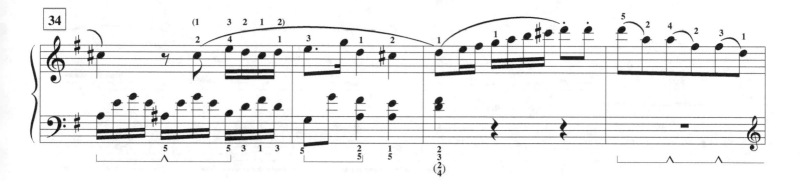

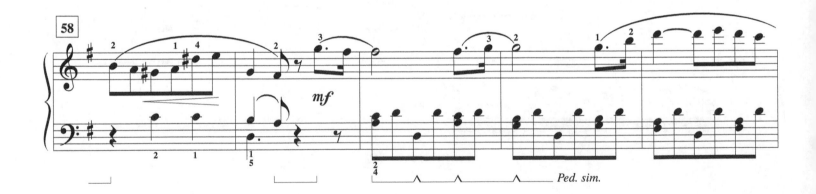

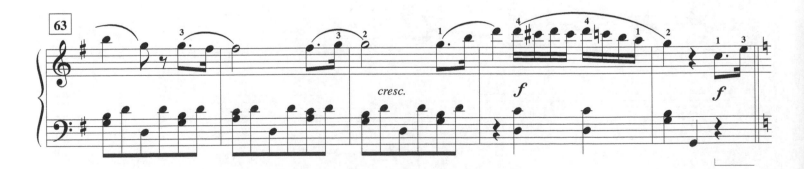

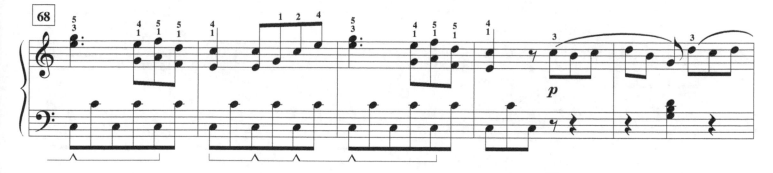

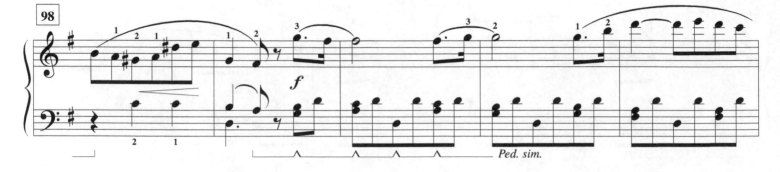

Exploring the Score: This movement is in **rondo** form. Find and label each section.

A   B   A   C   A   coda

(m. 28)

Sonata
K. 545

Wolfgang Amadeus Mozart
(1756-1791)

FF1113

74

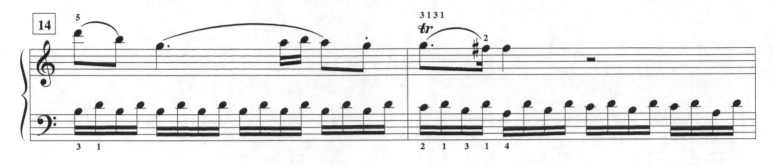

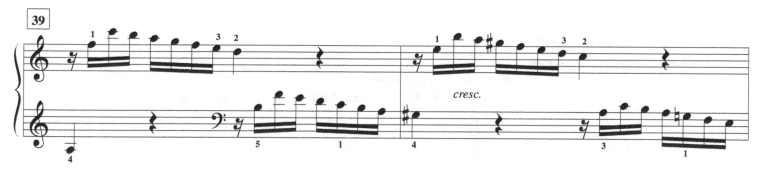

76

FF1113

System

Exploring the Score: Label the 1st and 2nd theme in the **exposition**. What is unusual about
the return of the 1st theme in the **recapitulation**?

- The theme is in minor. • The theme is in the dominant. • The theme is in the subdominant.

Andante

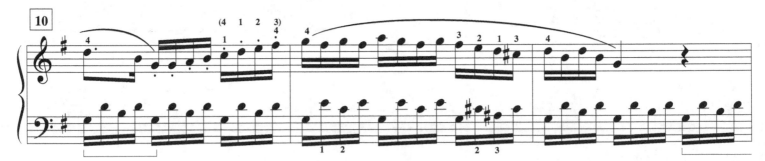

Hold the 5th finger to sustain the bass line.

80

FF1113

Exploring the Score: The first two pages of this movement are in **rounded binary form**.
Find and label each section in your music.

$\|:$ **A** **A¹** $:\|:$ **B** **A¹** $:\|$

Rondo

Allegretto

84

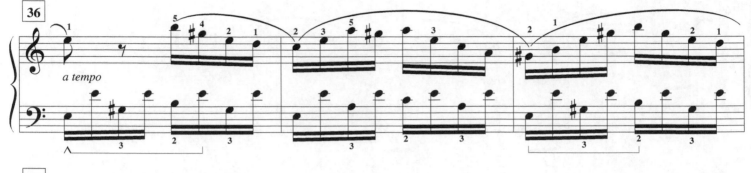

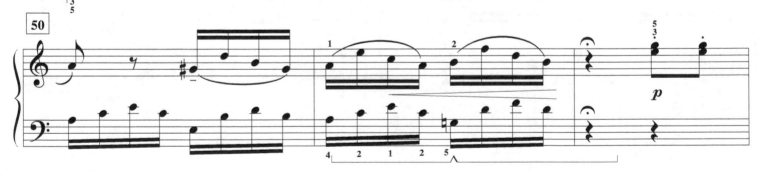

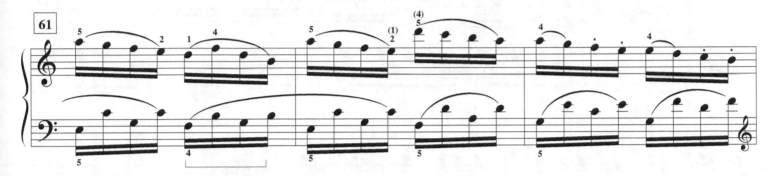

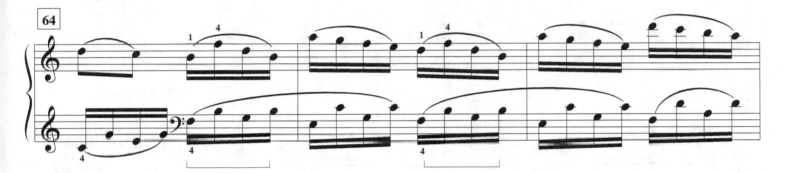

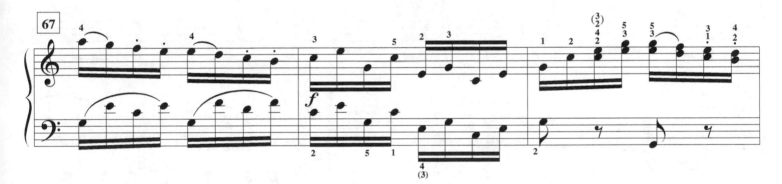

Exploring the Score: Where is the theme developed in the **relative minor** key?

Rondo à la Turk
(from Sonata in A Major, K. 331)

Wolfgang Amadeus Mozart
(1756-1791)

Allegretto

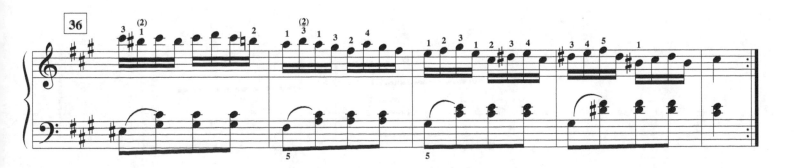

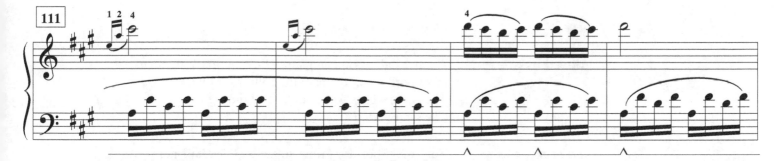

Exploring the Score: What is the form of *measures 1-24?* *(circle one)*

        binary   **rounded binary**   **ternary**

What is the form of *measures 33-56?*

        binary   **rounded binary**   **ternary**

DICTIONARY OF MUSICAL TERMS

Adagio	*Andante*	*Moderato*	*Allegretto*	*Allegro*	*Presto*
slowly	walking tempo	moderate tempo	rather fast	fast	very fast

SIGN	TERM	DEFINITION
>	**accent**	Play this note louder.
	Alberti bass	A left-hand accompaniment which outlines the notes of a chord using the pattern: bottom-top-middle-top. The Alberti bass was popularized during the Classical period.
¢	*alla breve*	Cut time. Short for $\frac{2}{2}$ time signature. The half note gets the beat.
	amoroso	Playfully.
	andantino	Literally, "little andante." Slightly faster than *andante*.
♪	*appoggiatura*	An ornament which looks like a grace note, but is played on the beat and shares the duration of the principal note. An appoggiatura resolves a dissonance to a consonance.
	arpeggio	Rolled chord. Play the notes of the chord one at a time, rapidly, from bottom to top.
	assai	Much. For example, *allegro assai* means "quite fast."
	a tempo	Return to the beginning tempo (speed).
	burlesco	A composition with a playful mood or character.
	cantabile	Singing.
	circa	About. For example, *circa* 1725 means approximately at that date.
	coda	Ending section. A short *coda* is called a *codetta*.
<	*crescendo (cresc.)*	Get gradually louder.
	con espressione	With expression.
	con spirito	With spirit.
	D.C. al Fine	*Da Capo al Fine.* Return to the beginning and play until *Fine* (end).

SIGN	TERM	DEFINITION
(decrescendo symbol)	*decrescendo*	Get softer. Same as *diminuendo*.
	development	The middle section of sonata-allegro form. Melodic fragments of the exposition themes are treated through modulations (changing keys) to build tension.
(diminuendo symbol)	*diminuendo (dim.)*	Get gradually softer.
	dolce	Sweetly.
	e	And (Italian). For example *cresc. e rit.*
espr.	*espressivo*	Expressively.
	exposition	The first section of sonata-allegro form. The exposition presents the 1st theme, 2nd theme, and an optional closing theme. In the classical sonanta the exposition repeats.
(fermata symbol)	*fermata*	Hold this note longer than usual.
	fp	*Forte* then *piano* (loud, immediately followed by soft.).
	Fine	End here.
fz	*forzando*	Forced, accented. Same as *sforzando*.
(grace note symbol)	**grace note**	A decorative note, written in small type. Grace notes are played quickly. Also called a *short appoggiatura,* the ornament is generally played on the beat for music of the Baroque and Classical periods. (See also *appoggiatura*.)
Hob.	**Hoboken**	Haydn's works do not have opus numbers. Consequently, the musicologist Hoboken researched and numbered them. Today we use the Hoboken numbers in listing the works of Haydn.
	il basso	In the bass.
	legato	Smoothly, connected.
	leggiero	Light and nimble.
	lento	Slowly; slower than *Adagio*.
	ma	But.
	marcato (marc.)	Marked; each note well articulated.

SIGN	TERM	DEFINITION
	meno	Less. For example, *meno mosso* means "less motion."
	minuet	A stately dance in $\frac{3}{4}$ time.
	molto	Very. For example, *molto rit.* means to take a big *ritard.*
	non troppo	Not too much. For example, *adagio non tropppo* means slowly, but not too slowly.
Op.	**opus**	Work. A composer's compositions are often arranged in sequence, with each work given an opus number. Several pieces may be included in a single opus. (Ex.: Op.3, No.1; Op.3, No.2, etc.)
	più mosso	More motion.
	poco a poco	Little by little.
	portato	Play in a slightly detached style. (Between legato and staccato.
	poco	A little.
rall.	**rallentando**	Gradually slow down. Same as *ritardando.*
	recapitulation	The restatement of the exposition, following the development. In the recapitulation, both 1st and 2nd themes are in the tonic key.
	risoluto	With firmness, decisiveness.
rit.	**ritardando**	Gradually slow down.
riten.	**ritenuto**	Slow down the tempo (immediately, not gradually).
	rondo	The form for a piece which has a recurring A Section. (Ex. ABACA)
	rubato	An expressive "give and take" of the tempo.
	sempre	Always. For example, *sempre staccato* means to continue playing staccato.
sfz or *sf*	*sforzando*	A sudden strong accent.
	simile	Similarly. Continue in the same way (same pedaling, same use of staccato, etc.).

SIGN	TERM	DEFINITION
	slur	Connect the notes within a slur.
	smorzando	Dying away. (Get softer.)
	sonata	Piece for solo piano, or solo instrument and piano. The classical sonata usually has 3 movements, the first in sonata-allegro form.
	sonata-allegro form	A musical form commonly used for first movements of sonatas, symphonies, quartets, etc. (See page 5.)
	sonatina	A little sonata.
	sostenuto	With a sustaining tone. Suggests a slightly slower tempo and a rich *legato*.
	spiritoso	With a spirited tempo.
	staccato	Play notes marked *staccato* detached, disconnected.
	staccato	The wedge was used by Beethoven and other early composers to indicate staccato.
	subito	Suddenly. For example, *subito piano* means suddenly soft.
	tempo	The speed of the music.
ten.	*tenuto*	Hold the note its full value.
	tenuto mark	Stress this note by pressing gently into the key.
	tre corda	Release the soft pedal. Literally, "three strings."
∞	**turn**	A musical ornament that "turns" above and below the given note.
tr	**trill**	A quick repetition of the principle note with the note above it. (The number and speed of the repetitions depend on the music.)
	una corda	Depress the soft pedal. Literally, "one string."
	vivace	Quickly, very lively.

ABOUT THE COMPOSERS

Ludwig van Beethoven (1770-1827)

Beethoven is one of the most well-known composers in history. He was born in
Germany and studied with Haydn in Vienna. In spite of severe hearing loss which
began in his mid 20's, Beethoven was a prolific composer. He even composed when
totally deaf, though the condition shortened his career as a performer and conductor.
His works include 9 symphonies, 32 piano sonatas, 5 piano concertos, numerous
chamber works, instrumental works, a ballet, an opera, other choral works, and 16
string quartets.

Muzio Clementi (1752-1832)

Clementi was a highly successful pianist and composer. He was born in Rome,
educated in England, and toured widely throughout Europe. He established a
publishing company and piano factory in England, and achieved lasting fame
with his compositions and exercises for piano students.

Cornelius Gurlitt (1820-1901)

As a young man, Gurlitt studied in Copenhagen, Denmark, and traveled throughout
Germany, Bohemia, Austria, and Italy. He taught at the Hamburg Conservatory and
composed choral, orchestral, and keyboard music. He is now best known for his
teaching pieces for the piano.

Franz Joseph Haydn (1732-1809)

Affectionately known as "Papa Haydn," this famous Austrian composer helped
develop the Classical style. He is known as the father of the symphony, and is
also responsible for bringing the string quartet into prominence. He composed
a vast number of pieces, including 60 piano sonatas.

Oswin Keller (1885-1928)

Oswin Keller studied and taught at the Leipzig Conservatory. Though he is not
widely known today, Keller wrote numerous pieces for the piano.

Friedrich Kuhlau (1786-1832)

Kuhlau was born in Germany and spent most of his life in Denmark. He was both a
concert pianist and prolific composer. Unfortunately, a fire in his home destroyed all
of his unpublished manuscripts and seriously affected his health. Nonetheless,
Kuhlau is famous for his many piano pieces and his popular compositions for flute.

Wolfgang Amadeus Mozart (1756-1791)

Mozart was a child prodigy who made his first public appearances at age 6 and had
his first compositions published at age 7. Wolfgang studied keyboard and violin with
his father Leopold Mozart, also a composer. Though he died at the early age of 35,
Wolfgang Amadeus Mozart left a legacy of nearly 50 symphonies, a dozen operas,
25 piano concertos, 42 violin sonatas, 23 string quartets, and 17 piano sonatas.